Fifteen Days of Faith

JOY MATHEWS

First printing 2017
Printed in the United States of America

Front & Back Cover Design by Kanika Harris
www.passionpgm.wix.com

Editor: Val Pugh-Love

ISBN: 9780692920213
Erica Joy Mathews Publishing

Visit www.amazon.com/author/joymathews
and
www.joymathews.com for purchases.

For booking, visit
www.joymathews.com/contact.

Acknowledgments

Right Now Faith

First, I have to thank God for keeping me when I didn't desire to hold on. He's the reason I *LIVE*, MOVE, BREATHE, and have my being. Thank you for giving me an extension on my life.

To my Superman, I thank you for being brave, helpful, and understanding. I love you more than words can express.

Mom and Dad, you have been here for my family and I throughout it all. Thank you for being so nurturing and loving. I love you both so much.

Thank you, Bishop and Co-Pastor Grant for praying for me and with me. I will ride off that faith whenever I must. I am a partaker of your grace. Hallelujah! I receive it, so I understand what access is available to me and for me.

Thanks to my sister Tina for yielding to become my angel throughout my fight with cancer.

To Carlos and Barbara Bates, thank you for coming by the house to sing to me and to pray for me. It has always filled my spirit with joy.

To my friend, Mary, thank you for showing me what friends are here for, you have been so supportive throughout my life - both good and bad. Thumbs up to my rider!

To the twins, I send you guys a big shout out for always making me laugh. I appreciate and love you two so much. Thanks for your love and care.

I want to send special thanks to my aunt Kathy for listening to me whenever I called for questions or concerns. I have always valued your opinion. Thanks and much love!

To Classy, you really encouraged me with all the texts. They all were heartfelt and inspiring. I know you meant well.

To Don Walls, my personal barber when I had to cut my long hair off, it was so hard, but you made me feel beautiful with my bald head. That's what childhood friends are for, and you're still here. Thanks!

To my kids, thanks for being here without question.

To my readers, thank all of you for your support. Thank you and much love in Jesus name!

Joy Mathews

Introduction

"Now faith is the substance of things hoped for,
the evidence of things not seen."
Hebrews 11:1

God gave each of us a measure of faith. You must eat the word daily in order for your seed to produce. Hebrews 11:6 says, "Without faith it is impossible to please Him: for he that comes to God must believe that he is, and that he is a rewarder of them that diligently seek him." I encourage you to be real in your faith walk. When I was diagnosed with seventeen tumors on my brain, I remember telling a friend to stop crying. My words to her were, "Don't you dare breakdown on me. I don't need weak people around me. You've got to be strong." Immediately she strengthened, and God began to move. She fell to her knees and the Holy Ghost fell on both of us. He quickened my spirit to write *15 Days of Faith* to inspire the weak and make them strong.

This book is all about right now faith. When tragedy, mayhem, death, and destruction become eminent, yesterday's faith won't do. We need right now faith! So many Christians are not living in the right now faith. As a result, they are not seeing God's work at hand in their lives. We believe God for our eternal salvation but not our sanctification or what I like to call "right here, right now, everyday faith." The writer of Hebrews states, "NOW FAITH" is the substance of things hoped for. Right now faith does not wait on healing, deliverance, mercy, grace, love, and the prosperity of God. Right now faith believes that we already have it. We don't just talk about it; we walk it out.

It is an overflowing faith journey that takes us over the top and moves in the right direction for the power of the Holy Spirit. This faith reaches out to the sick, homeless, battered, and imprisoned. It believes the blind will see, the deaf will hear, and the lame will walk. It believes the impossible. Our right now faith understands that the same power that raised Jesus from the dead can heal cancer and all sickness and disease. It can and will save the lost and bring light to the darkest soul. We can't allow the enemy to lie, cheat, or steal our faith through cunningness, deceit, trickery, and deception. Our God is the same God yesterday, today, and forever. We believe we are healed, saved, and redeemed by the blood of Jesus RIGHT NOW!

$\mathcal{D}ay$ 1

Song: "I Need Thee Every Hour"
by Bishop Paul Morton

"Now faith is the substance of things hoped for,
the evidence of things not seen."
Hebrews 11:1

Right now faith is the substance, matter, and essence of who we place our hope in and what we hope for. It is the evidence, proof, confirmation, verification, and fact of who we are in and through Christ. Faith forward, next-level thinkers are men and women of God who wholeheartedly move in the direction and operation of the Holy Spirit. If God says it, we believe it.

"[1] Fret not thyself because of evildoers, neither
be thou envious against the workers of inequity.
[2] For they shall soon be cut down like the grass,
and wither as the green herb."
Psalm 37:1-2

When we fret, worry, fuss, and trouble ourselves with evildoers, we are playing right into the hands of the enemy. This will always hold us bound with fear, which is the opposite of faith. When we are concerned with what they are doing, then we cannot focus on what we need to do in the Lord. Being envious of the workers of iniquity takes us to a place of jealousy and strife towards people who are evil and sinful; thus, making us no better than they are. Every day we must strive to keep our faith focused on God and all of His glorious promises.

Prayer and Meditation

O, God, we believe. Help our unbelief, God. You place our faith in the right object, the right area, the right subject, and the right direction. Lead and guide our lives, our hands, and our ministries through your Holy Ghost. O, that you would bless us indeed and enlarge our territories. Expand our faith, our spiritual discernment, and the spiritual content in our hearts, minds, bodies, and souls. Lift us to the highest planes, to our next levels, into the third heaven, and propel our faith into the unknown through the marvelous light of your Son Jesus the Christ. In Jesus' name! Amen!

Day 2

Song: "I Need You Now"
by Smokie Norful

"I am crucified with Christ: nevertheless, I live;
yet not I, but Christ liveth in me; and the life
which I now live in the flesh I live by faith of the
Son of God,
who love me and gave himself for me."
Galatians 2:20

The power of Christ that dwells in us
creates a path of true influence, authority, and
control. It creates a power to live, to overcome, to
conquer, and to defeat the enemy. Because we are
crucified with Christ, we also live, and He lives
in us. The flesh is dead, but our faith in Jesus
opens the doors to our newfound spiritual life – a
life of abundance, wealth, health, and love.

"Trust in the Lord and do good;
so shall thou dwell in the land, and verily thou
shall be fed."
Psalm 37:3

Trust, faith, belief, hope, dependence, reliance, expectation, and confidence are necessary in our daily lives. When we put our trust in the Lord and do the good that He has for us, we will begin to see the fruits of our labor and be fed daily by His word. Nothing shall stop us from what God is doing in our lives. So many times, we have trusted in people and things other than God and the people that He has put in our lives. As we gain confidence in Him, we begin to see the manifestation of His glory in our situations, circumstances, and the people that God is introducing to us and our ministries. We must have a loftier element of faith than the common men or women of faith that are just in the church and not of the church.

Prayer and Meditation

O, My God, our healer, redeemer, and deliverer… We put our trust in you. We depend on you. Our faithful expectations are in you, and you are the provision for our lives. Feed our faith, O God. Take us out of the flesh, lift us in the Spirit, and set our feet on higher ground. O Lord, in the name of Jesus, we speak peace, prosperity, wealth, affluence, and success in our lives, relationships, families, businesses, and ministries. We claim ultimate power over sin and death in our lives. We believe by the power of your Holy Ghost that our enemies are our footstools, and we release your blessing, abundance, and profusion in the atmosphere. In Jesus' name! Amen!

Day 3

Song: "For Your Glory"
by Tasha Cobbs

"16 That He would grant you, according to the riches of His glory, to be strengthened with might and by His Spirit in the inner man; 17 that Christ might dwell in your hearts by faith; that ye being rooted and grounded in love, 18 May be able to comprehend with all saints what is the breadth, and length, and the depth, and height; 19 and to know the love of Christ, which passeth knowledge, that ye might be filled with the fullness of God. 20 Now unto him that is able to do exceeding abundantly above all that we can ask or think, according to the power that worketh in us 21 Unto him be the glory in the church by Christ Jesus throughout all ages, world without end. Amen."
Ephesians 3:16-21

We are joined together in faith; strengthened by His power and might. We have the full capacity of His Spirit working in and through us. Our faith is to the max but cannot and will not be maxed out. We are not afraid to put our faith forward in overdrive and smash the gas. Love will plant us and enforce our will to walk in all the fullness of our calling. We are saved, sanctified, and washed in the blood. We are King's kids, members of a royal priesthood, and our abundance is coming.

> *"Delight thyself also in the Lord; and he shall give thee the desires of thine heart."*
> *Psalm 37:4*

Delight, enjoy, take pleasure, and be happy in the Lord, and His desires will become our desires. When His desire burns in our hearts, minds, and souls, we will take our faith lives into a new dimension. Then, the trajectory and range of what we can accomplish will take us into the spiritual orbit unknown to the natural man. To be delighted in the Lord is an extremely profound emotion that produces an unspeakable pleasure with total gratification. It is always aroused by deep desire found in the faith of what God is already doing and what He will continue to do in and through our lives.

Prayer and Meditation

Gracious and Mighty Father of all things, you have all the power, all the riches, and all the glory. Move, make room, and take control of all that we do. Help us, O God. Implant your desires in us. We claim peace, love, and prosperity in our lives. We release your power in our relationships and ministries. Increase, overflow, and move as we proclaim your everlasting gospel. Reach deep inside of our inner being and fill us with your Spirit that we may achieve, attain, and complete our mission through you. Show us your desire for our lives. Give us our desires. God, we claim victory, triumph, and conquest in everything we do. Continue to unite our souls, strengthen our hands for the battle, and prepare our hearts to encounter even the deepest profound experiences that we endeavor to assemble. God, we know that we can do all things through Christ who strengthens us. In Jesus' name! Amen!

Day 4

"[11] Where unto we are appointed, preachers, and apostles, and teachers of the Gentiles. [12] For the which cause we also suffer these things; nevertheless, I am not ashamed: for we know that whom we have believed and am persuaded that he is able to keep that which we have committed unto Him against that day. [13] Holdfast the form of sound words, which you hast heard of us in faith and love which is in Christ Jesus. [14] That good thing which was committed unto thee kept by the Holy Ghost which dwells in us."
2 Timothy 1:11-14

While commitment is a fundamental and principle function of our faith, it always seems to be the place we struggle the most. In order to be elitist in Christ, being committed is paramount. Committed faith stands strong. We may sway and bend, but we never break. Strong commitment keeps us on our knees longer, in our word longer, and on the battlefield until the enemy is defeated.

Because we are committed to Jesus, we are bound and bonded together through His blood. Faith is no good without commitment, because commitment is the glue that seals our faith. It is the proof positive that we are who we say we are. Jesus was committed to the Father, so shall we continue to be committed to Him that we may know the will of the Father and be given the power to carry it out.

"⁵ Commit thy way unto the Lord; trust also in him and he shall bring it to pass. ⁶ And he shall bring forth thy righteousness as the light and thy judgment as the noonday.
Psalm 37:5-6

We are morally bound, charged, obligated, and pledged to the Lord. We have a duty to Him, His word, precepts, plans, and the progress of His purpose for our lives. When we are totally committed not just in word, but indeed in our work, ways, and will, putting our full faith and trust in Him, His will, and His purpose and plans for us will come to pass. He will bring forth His righteousness in us and shine His light not only to our path, but also to a dark and dying world through us.

Prayer and Meditation

O, my God, you are so Holy, so mighty, and so awesome in power. Your presence in our life, ministry, and in every intricate fact of our day is so forceful, influential, potent, and persistent. God, we commit every degree of our being to you. We totally dedicate 100% of ourselves, our hearts, minds, bodies, and souls to you, your purpose, and your plan for our lives. In the name of Jesus, bring peace, love, happiness, and prosperity to us, our families, our ministries, and relationships. Allow your light to shine as bright as the sun. God, we praise and worship you. We give you all the glory and the entire honor. In Jesus' name! Amen!

Day 5

Song: "Fill Me Up/Overflow"
by Tasha Cobbs

"[21] And having a high priest over the house of God. [22] Let us draw near with a true heart in full assurance of faith having our hearts sprinkled from an evil conscience, and our bodies washed with pure water. [23] Let us hold fast the profession of our faith without wavering for he is faithful that promised [24] And let us consider one another to provoke and (stir up) unto love and to good works."
Hebrews 10:21-24

We must have a corresponding, well-balance symmetry in our faith and action. Our witness is only as strong as our walk. Our testimony is only as good as our test. And, sometimes our test is just simply to rest. Our rest draws us nearer to Him and activates or brings life to what we believe. We become living, eating, breathing, sleeping, walking, talking, faith men and women that are in constant motion moving towards what we believe. Faith inspires, moves, and motivates. It is the muscle behind our every action in Christ. The most profound difference between *good* men and women of faith and *great* men and women of faith is not just what they believe they can do, but what they actually do. Faith must produce! When it calls, we must get up and move. Stretched out stellar - even sometimes stealth-like faith - is a must. We must be sold out, signed, sealed, and delivered. It is what we do, who we are, and where we are going in through the blood of Jesus.

"Rest in Lord and wait patiently for Him: fret not thyself because of him who prospers in his way, because of the man who bringeth wicked devices to pass."
Psalm 37:7

Resting in our faith sounds like sitting idle, relaxing, and doing nothing. However, resting in Jesus is a progressive process that is everything but idle. By resting in Jesus, we have an assurance of love, peace, prosperity, joy, and happiness. Yes, we have entered into His rest. Now our reliance is in what He accomplished at the cross. Furthermore, resting regenerates, activates, motivates, and coordinates our faith in the right direction. It produces, promotes, and pushes us to the next level in Him. When we see the enemy prospering, it is so easy for us to worry and lose our patience. However, wicked devices will fail, but love never fails.

Prayer and Meditation

O, my God of power, God of might, God of wisdom, we rest in you, your ways, and in your holiness, your plan, and purpose for our life. Though the enemy seems to prosper in the way, we fret not, for we know our redeemer lives. God, we understand and rest in your promise for love and happiness. We know that your plans shall come to pass; we know that you are in control and trust your timing. Give us strength, O Lord, to gain knowledge, wisdom, and understanding in our rest. Take us higher in and through you. In Jesus' name! Amen!

Day 6

Song: "Take Me to the King"
by Tamela Mann

"When Jesus heard it, he marveled, and said to them that followed, verily I say unto you, I have not found so great faith, no, not in Israel."
Matthew 8:10

When our faith steps out, Jesus steps in. His power, salvation, deliverance, and healing shows up and shows out. When we cease from self and put our best faith forward, it gives God the opportunity to move in and through our situations and circumstances. We must remember that faith is a progressive process. It is not our motion and movement. Rather, it is the cause and effect of our movement or the lack thereof. Faith is not the life, the blood, or the air itself. Instead, it is the heartbeat and the lungs that pump the oxygen in and out and allows us to live the life we love and long for.

"Cease from anger, and forsake wrath: fret not thyself in any wise to do evil."
Psalm 37:8

God is constantly warning us to stay away from anger and wrath. He has told us not to worry and to steer clear of evil. This was hard even for some of the greatest and most faith-filled men and women in the bible. The keywords in the scripture are *cease*, *forsake*, and *fret not*. When troubles come your way, stand still; don't worry about it. Now, that takes patient faith to do so, but it is not impossible. A solid man or woman of faith will stand still and know that he belongs to God.

Prayer and Meditation

Dear Heavenly Father, you are so Holy. God, we stand in awe of you. We know that your hand will move. We seek your face, your love, your fellowship, and your comfort. Therefore, we see your hand moving in and through all that you do in our lives, love, family, relationships, and ministries. Continue to articulate your love and power over our lives, and move with abundance. In Jesus' name! Amen!

Day 7

**Song: "I Give Myself Away"
by William McDowell**

*"¹³ In whom ye also trusted, after that ye heard
the word of truth, the gospel of your salvation:
in whom also after that ye believe, ye were
sealed with that Holy Spirit of promise ¹⁴ Which
is the earnest of our inheritance until the
redemption of the purchased possession, unto
the praise of his glory."
Ephesians 1:13-14*

Trusting in what God has promised will
bring forth power to attain our eternal
inheritance, as well as our right-here-right-now
inheritance. We have been redeemed, saved,
sanctified, set apart, and set free by the blood of
the Lamb. Our inheritance is so massive, so vast,
and so colossal that the human mind cannot
comprehend or fathom its span. God is calling us
into our place of wealth, health, and success. This
wealth cannot be measured with worldly material,
and temporal goods. Our inheritance is a
supernatural unending expense. However, it is

just as real in this life and in this world as it is in the next.

"⁹ For evildoers shall be cut off: but those that wait upon the Lord, they shall inherit the earth. ¹⁰ For yet a little while, and the wicked shall not be: yea, thou shalt diligently consider his place, and it shall not be. ¹¹ But the meek inherit the earth; and shall delight themselves in the abundance of peace."
Psalm 37:9-11

The inheritance that God has for us is ours and no one can take it away. There is a relatively unknown dimension that must be understood in order to fully partner with God and experience the fullness of His blessing, which is His inheritance. It is the unseen realm of the spirit. It is invisible yet real, hidden, and active. Much of what happens in our blessed life here on earth is influenced by it - certainly anything of eternal significance or which controls, shapes, and molds our destiny. God is bringing us into a new dimension in our lives, relationships, families, and ministries. We must enforce, implement, and impose the will of God in every facet of our lives. With perfect precision, He is moving us towards our inheritance.

Prayer and Meditation

O Holy and wonderful, glorious Father, you alone are the master of the universe. God, we trust and put our full faith in you. In the mighty name of Jesus, we claim and proclaim, even declare unto the heavens and here on earth that we take possession of our inheritance. We stand on the promises you have made unto us. God, we take authority over any satanic or demonic powers that may be hindering us from taking possession of all that you have for us. Right now, God, we claim victory, peace, love, joy, and happiness in our lives. In the name of Jesus! Amen!

Day 8

**Song: "Because of Who You Are"
by Vicki Yohe**

*"Above all taking the shield of faith wherewith
ye shall be able to quench all the fiery darts of
the wicked."
Ephesians 6:16*

How big, strong, wide, mighty, powerful,
stout, and sturdy is our shield! Our faith in Jesus
and what He has already accomplished at the
cross must be stalwart and capable of exerting
considerable effort while withstanding difficult
stress and hardships. Faith-forward, next-level
men and women of faith have shields that possess
the highest concentration of the distinguishing
ingredients that are needed. No matter how
inflammatory the darts of the enemy are, we are
able to withstand. Struggling is a part of the
process. No one said it would be easy, but I heard
someone say that anything worth having is worth
fighting for. Love, life, peace, healing, joy, and
true life-fulfilling happiness come with a price. In
our case, the price was paid at Calvary. The
question is: Are we willing to walk by faith?

"12 The wicked plotteth against the just, and gnasheth upon him with his teeth. 13 The Lord shall laugh at him: for he sees that his day is coming. 14 The wicked have drawn out the sword, and have bent their bow, to cast down the poor and needy, and to slay such as be of upright conversation. 15 Their sword shall enter into their own heart, and their bows shall be broken. 16 A little that a righteous man hath is better than the riches of many wicked. 17 For the arms of the wicked shall be broken; but the Lord upholdeth the righteous."
Psalm 37:12-17

We often ask: Why me? Why us, Lord? The Lord says, *why not us…* Our faith in action is determined by every knee jerk reaction, spur of the moment, or carefully considered response that we make toward the devices of the enemy. Knowing that God has our back, moving forward becomes second nature. Even in our darkest times, His light shines. The great Martin Luther King said, "The true character (faith) of a man (or woman) is evident when he or she is faced with their greatest adversity." Now is the time to be faithful and press forward.

Prayer and Meditation

O Lord, our God, King, and Master of what and who we are, you have created us in your own image. Grant us wisdom, knowledge, and understanding that we may continue to withstand anything the enemy tries to throw our way. Help us by strengthening our shield of faith that you may shield us from his fiery darts. God of power and might, sickness and disease has no power over sin and death you have destroyed. Your overcoming power is released in our lives. We profess it, confess it, and decree victory in the name of Jesus! Amen!

Day 9

**Song: "Jesus Loves Me"
by Whitney Houston**

*"The thief cometh not, but for to steal, and to
kill, and to destroy: I am come that they might
have life, and that they might have it more
abundantly."*
John 10:10

A life of abundance is a life full of faith.
There is no way to accomplish and acquire
abundance of life, love, and happiness in this life
or the life to come without faith. The devil is
constantly trying to steal our joy, peace, love,
happiness, and healing. He wants to kill our life,
body, and hope. He would like nothing more than
to destroy our faith and especially our testimony.
But God! He has promised an abundant life - a
life where wealth and love reigns supreme! The
Lord our God shepherds us, comforts us, and
protects us. We already have abundance! All we
have to do is walk and live in it!

[18] The LORD knows the days of the upright, and their inheritance shall be forever. [19] They shall not be ashamed in the evil time, and in the days of famine they shall be satisfied. [20] But the wicked shall perish; And the enemies of the LORD, Like the splendor of the meadows, shall vanish. Into smoke they shall vanish away. [21] The wicked borrows and does not repay, but the righteous shows mercy and gives. [22] For those blessed by Him shall inherit the earth, but those cursed by Him shall be cut off.
Psalm 37:18-22

When we place our faith in whom we have our righteousness, we receive, live, breathe, walk, and talk as men and women who have full confidence in our inheritance. Our inheritance is life more abundantly. In this life, we are completely satisfied. When evil times come, we will not be ashamed for we know who we are and whose we are. By inheriting the earth, God is calling us to a higher degree of faith that will allow us to subdue the enemy and win souls for Christ. It will also enable us to live a life of righteousness and be blessed in the land, blessed going out, and blessed coming in. We are the head and not the tail. We are the lender and not the borrower. We have a harvest of plenty, and we are blessed in the city where we must count the few as many.

Prayer and Meditation

Holy and righteous God, God of
abundance, build our faith. Make us strong, and
lift us higher. God, according to your wealth of
grace and your mercy, reveal your plan. Show us
your ways so that we can become kingdom
builders of this day and age. God, you are the
architect of your kingdom. Make us wise,
knowledgeable, solid foundation builders and
brick and mortar masons for your kingdom. Bless
us to the fullest. Strengthen our hearts and renew
our minds that we may flourish. Give us health,
wealth, and life. Rain down your mercy and
grace on our families, our finances, our children,
our ministries, and our relationships. God, we
need your latter rain, we need your increase, and
we need your power. We believe it and receive it
right now. In the name of Jesus! Amen!

Day 10

Song: "You Deserve It"
by J.J. Hairston & Youthful Praise

"For we walk by faith, not by sight. [7] We are always confident, knowing that whilst we are at home in the body, we are absent from the Lord; [8] We are confident I say and willing rather to be absent from the body, and to be present with the Lord. [9] Wherefore we labor, that whether present and or absent, we may be accepted of him."
2 Corinthians 5:7-9

This walk of faith cannot and will not rely on our five natural senses. We cannot taste it, smell it, hear it, feel it, or see it within our natural faculties; it is purely supernatural in substance. However, the supernatural can and will activate, motivate, and populate the natural sense. And, if given the rule and reign, it will dominate the physical life to the degree of total submission. Our faith must come to the ultimate conclusion of power, love, and of a sound mind wired and ready for action. It stands strong in the face of adversity and compromises with no failure. Therefore, our faith is constant in victory, leaving all on the field of battle. Death has no rule and sin no value.

"The steps of a good man are ordered by the Lord: and he delighteth in his way. Though he falls, he shall not be utterly cast down: for the Lord upholdeth him in his hand."
Psalm 37:23-24

When we claim every step in perfect precision with the divine order of God's prescribed, prearranged, and approved plan and purpose for our lives, we make God happy. At this point, it is impossible to fail. Our direction is sure, our vision is clear, and our function is explicit and determined. We discover that we are virtually victorious in everything we do. Even when we fall, we are held up by His mighty hand.

Prayer and Meditation

Awesome, mighty, wonderful, and Holy Father of heaven and earth, in the name of Jesus, order our every step, order our walk, and our talk. Shape us, mold us, and make us into the men and women that you have called us to be in and through your word, your ways, and your perfect will for our life, love, and ministry. Take us into the spiritual stratosphere and the higher plans of holiness for your namesake. God, today we claim victory in every aspect of our lives. We claim healing, deliverance, wealth, health, and love now and forever. Use us, O God, for your plan, purpose, and promise. In Jesus' name! Amen!

Day 11

Song: "Victory Belongs to Jesus"
by Todd Dulaney

"¹ Therefore, being justified by faith, we have
peace with God through our Lord Jesus Christ:
² By whom also we have access by faith into this
grace wherein we stand and rejoice in hope of
the glory of God."
Romans 5:1-2

The fact that we have been justified,
saved, and sanctified by the faith we have in
Jesus gives us total access to the throne room of
God. Now we are able to stand. When trouble
comes and we feel like lying down and giving up,
Jesus is right there to pick us up and put our feet
on higher ground. We continue to bask in His
glory, receiving healing, power, deliverance,
mercy, and grace to live a life rich and
prosperous in and through Jesus.

"²⁵ I have been young, and now am old; yet have
not seen the righteous forsaken, nor his seed

begging for bread. [26] He is ever merciful, and lendeth; and his seed is blessed."
Psalm 37:25-26

Because we have received the righteousness of God, we cannot and will not at any point be forsaken, nor will our descendants beg for bread. We are blessed by the best, placing our faith solely and exclusively in the righteousness of Jesus. He placed us in position for prosperity, and because we prosper, everyone we come in contact with is blessed. The power of the Holy Ghost is so rich and pure in and through our lives, and we spread joy, peace, love, and happiness to all.

Prayer and Meditation

God, you said that you would supply all that we need according to your riches and glory. God, we need you to supply abundance that we may saturate the earth with your work, your ways, your word, and your will. According to your riches and your power, our blessings were given to us that we may be a blessing to your people. God, give us wisdom, knowledge, and understanding that we may use the abundance which you have given us for your work and our ministries. In Jesus' name! Amen!

Day 12

Song: "I Don't Mind Waiting"
by Juanita Bynum

"But without faith it is impossible to please him;
for he that cometh to God must believe that he
is, and that he is a rewarder of them that
diligently seek him."
Hebrews 11:6

Love is and always will be the game changer. Faith and hope are the twin towers that solidify our law to and from God and one another. All three must work in a perfect unison together. However, in no way, can it work if love is not the prevailing factor. Love must be paramount, dominant, and the primary driving force behind our faith and hope. It moves God because love is God and God is love. There is no way to separate the two, and there is no way to truly love or be loved with or by anyone without the ordination of the love of God. Love is the most powerful force on earth and in heaven. Its evil twin - hate - while a force to be reckoned with, cannot and will not overcome love. Love is the conquering giant with its extraordinary power. It will win; it never fails.

"27 Depart from evil, and do good; and dwell for evermore. 28 For the LORD loveth judgment, and forsaketh not his saints; they are preserved for ever: but the seed of the wicked shall be cut off."
Psalm 37:27-28

Faith shows up in our lives, and then we become men and women that operate in a different field. It is as if we are in a bubble to the world – a bubble that cannot be penetrated by any force that moves in a worldly atmosphere. We are in the world but not of the world. We battle not against flesh and blood but against powers, principalities, and spiritual wickedness in high places. We please God with our faith, and we make the enemy tremble. Thank God that as we diligently seek Him, He continues to reward us. There must be a departure (the act of leaving) from evil. When we are obedient servants to God, we are preserved for prosperity. He has given us a vision for victory, and we must continue to conquer and believe for our benefits.

Prayer and Meditation

O God of love and power, we know that you are calling us to a higher calling and a higher love through who and what you are. God, help us to depart from any evil that may be hindering and interfering with the progress that keeps us from attaining and accomplishing true love, life, and happiness through you. God, show us your love. Open the heavens and rain down your love on us. God, preserve us for prosperity, open our vision for victory that we may continue to conquer and believe for our benefits in your precious blood. In the name of Jesus! Amen!

Day 13

Song: "You're Bigger"
by Jekalyn Carr

"By faith Abraham when he was called to go out into a place which he should after receive for an inheritance, obeyed; and he went out, not knowing whither he went."
Hebrews 11:8

Now, this is a supremely excellent and impeccable picture of blind faith. God called Abraham, and he responded. God said he would receive, and Abraham believed it was so. Abraham's obedience to God is unprecedented in the Old testament. When we hear the voice of God, we must move and put our full faith forward just as he did. No matter how impossible the situation may seem, God will see us through to our full inheritance. If God promised it, He will perform it!

"29 The righteous shall inherit the land, and dwell therein forever. 30 The mouth of the

righteous speaketh wisdom, and his tongue
talketh of judgment. [31] The law of his God is in
his heart; none of his steps shall slide. [32] The
wicked watcheth the righteous, and seeketh to
slay him. [33] The LORD will not leave him in his
hand, nor condemn him when he is judged. [34]
Wait on the LORD, and keep his way, and he
shall exalt thee to inherit the land: when the
wicked are cut off, thou shalt see it."
Psalm 37:29-34

Abraham believed God and counted on
Him for righteousness. He never asked any
questions; he just moved with well-balanced
poised, and prolific precision. Every step he took
was directed by God. Therefore, his steps did not
slide or slip. We must learn from the Father of
our faith. If God promised it, we believe it and
receive it.

Prayer and Meditation

God, we believe in your promise and our
inheritance. We walk in faith and not doubt. We
will not stagger at your promise of love, life,
happiness, healing, peace, and prosperity. God,
we bind the hand of the enemy and anything that
may be trying to keep us from whatever you have
already promised to us. We release your Spirit in
our lives, our families, relationships, and

ministries through your word, ways, and perfect will for our lives. Thank you for your love, healing, deliverance, and inheritance. In Jesus's name! Amen!

Day 14

Song: "I Smile"
by Kirk Franklin

"He replied, "Because you have so little faith.
Truly I tell you, if you have faith as small as a
mustard seed, you can say to this mountain,
'Move from here to there,' and it will move.
Nothing will be impossible for you."
Matthew 17:20

There are so many mountains in our lives
that seem to always be getting in our way. Doubt,
fear, depression, sickness, and loneliness are
linked to unbelief, sin, and death. Nevertheless,
just a small amount of faith tends to turn our
situations around and set our feet on higher
ground. There is no way for us to win the
constant daily battle against the forces of evil
unless we speak to our mountain. The problem is
sometimes we are so blinded by foolish pride and
selfish ambitions that we refuse to identify the
mountains in our lives. Sometimes we try to go
around the mountains in our lives. Other times,

we try to climb those mountains. But, Jesus told us to say, "Mountain, get out of my way and be removed from my life!" Release your faith into the atmosphere, and God will move the mountain. As a result, we will receive our victory.

"[35] I have seen the wicked in great power, and spreading himself like a green bay tree. [36] Yet he passed away, and, lo, he was not: yea, I sought him, but he could not be found. [37] Mark the perfect man, and behold the upright: for the end of that man is peace. [38] But the transgressors shall be destroyed together: the end of the wicked shall be cut off."
Psalm 37:35-38

When we are awakened to full faith, no doubt God has bloomed in our hearts, minds, and souls. As men and women of God, we are called to a higher standard. We are in the perfect; therefore, we are made perfect in His blood. Faith feet run, jump, climb, and walk with purpose. Furthermore, just as David, we dance before the Lord. We are King's kids - holy, separated, and set apart for His work and His will. We dare not doubt, but always dare to dream big. We are confident, never cocky, but always certain by the blood of the lamb.

Prayer and Meditation

Thank you, O God, for the power of the Holy Ghost. Thank you for the treasure chest of faith, hope, and love and for the peace and prosperity. You are our King, Lord, and Savior. Continue to strengthen our hearts, minds, and souls so that our hands may be used for your work and our feet for the work of the gospel. In the name of Jesus! Amen!

Day 15

Song: "Faith" by J. Moss

"Therefore, we are buried with him by baptism into death: that like as Christ was raised up from the dead by the glory of the Father, even so we also should walk in the newness of life."
Romans 6:4

Faith is knowing fully that we have died, been buried, and has already resurrected with Christ who lives in us. Everything we say and do is by the will of the Father because Christ is our everything. We live, eat, breathe, and sleep as men and women of God. We are Christ people, and we move and operate under the authority of the Holy Ghost. Because of our relationship with Him, we find ourselves believing and receiving the impossible.

"[39] But the salvation of the righteous is of the LORD: he is their strength in the time of trouble. [40] And the LORD shall help them, and deliver them: he shall deliver them from the

wicked, and save them, because they trust in him."
Psalm 37:39-40

Paul said in Philippians 3:9, "And being found in Him, not having mine own righteousness, which is of the law, but that which is through the faith of Christ, the righteousness which is of God by faith." Thank God, we don't have to depend on our own righteousness, which is of the law. Instead, we have faith in the righteousness that Jesus provides for us. Now that gives us strength and power because we have the help that we need when we trust and have confidence in Jesus, the author and finisher of our faith. We must put our full faith forward with explosive resilience as we walk through life with our Savior.

Prayer and Meditation

O God, you reign supreme in every aspect and feature of our lives. Thank you for your healing power, your strength when we feel weak, and the power that you give us to be overcomers. We are more than conquerors through your blood. God, we take authority over all powers that may try to hinder us from approaching your throne of grace and mercy. We bind anything that may try to rise against us and our ministries. We claim victory in our lives, in our children's lives, and in our relationships. In the name of Jesus! Amen!

About the Author

Erica "Joy" Mathews is a native of Shreveport, Louisiana. She is a loving wife and wonderful mother of three children. The name "Joy" describes her well, and it shows through the love that she bestows upon everyone she meets. She found Christ in 2004. Through her passion in prison ministry and her love for God and others, she has led many to Christianity. She is a member of the Greater New Zion FGBC of Shreveport, LA where she is a minister and remains focused, fervent, and faithful in her walk with Christ.

She received her Associates Degree at Southern University of Shreveport in 2002. This phenomenal entrepreneur woman has owned an array of businesses, and she is an active author, speaker, and business consultant. Joy's strong will, sophistication, and drive will push you into purpose. Moreover, her undeniable faith, passion, and belief that with God all things are possible led her to write her debut books *The devil Almost Won, But God* and *15 Days of Faith*.